Ladybird  Readers

Bumblebee and the Rock Concert

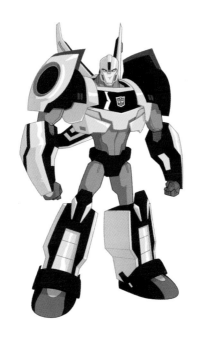

Picture words

 Russell

Denny

Autobots

Bumblebee

Strongarm

Grimlock

Fixit

Ladybird  Readers

Bumblebee and the Rock Concert

Series Editor: Sorrel Pitts
Adapted by Hazel Geatches

LADYBIRD BOOKS

UK | USA | Canada | Ireland | Australia
India | New Zealand | South Africa

Ladybird Books is part of the Penguin Random House group of companies
whose addresses can be found at global.penguinrandomhouse.com.
www.penguin.co.uk   www.puffin.co.uk   www.ladybird.co.uk

First published 2017
001

Printed in China

A CIP catalogue record for this book is available from the British Library

ISBN: 978-0-241-29867-1

All correspondence to
Ladybird Books
Penguin Random House Children's
80 Strand, London WC2R 0RL

MIX
Paper from
responsible sources
FSC® C018179

Bisk

Decepticons

cable

scrapyard

soundboard

rock concert

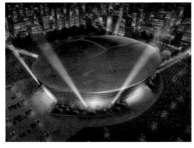

Rumbledome

stage

One Friday night, the Autobots were in the city, looking for Decepticons.

"The Decepticons want cables to get strong. We must find the cables. Then, we can find the Decepticons, and stop them," said Bumblebee.

Grimlock looked in a train and found a cable.

But a Decepticon hit Grimlock
and took it.

Bumblebee and Strongarm tried
to catch the Decepticon, but he
jumped on to a moving train.

"Ha, ha! I've got the cable!"
he laughed.

The Autobots went back to Denny's scrapyard, where Denny and Russell waited for them.

"You're all very tired. You must sleep," said Denny.

"No, we can't sleep. The Decepticons are taking all the cables. We must stop them," said Bumblebee.

Then, Fixit had an idea. "The Decepticons want soundboards, too," he said. "There is a rock concert at the Rumbledome tomorrow night. There are always lots of soundboards at rock concerts."

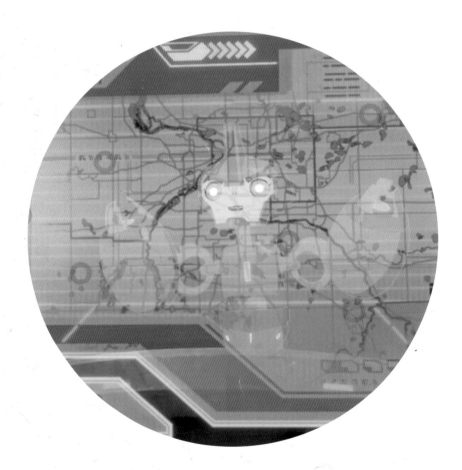

"Why do the Decepticons want cables and soundboards?" asked Russell.

"They can use them to get strong," said Bumblebee.

"We must go to the rock concert to stop the Decepticons," said Bumblebee. "And there is a great band playing!"

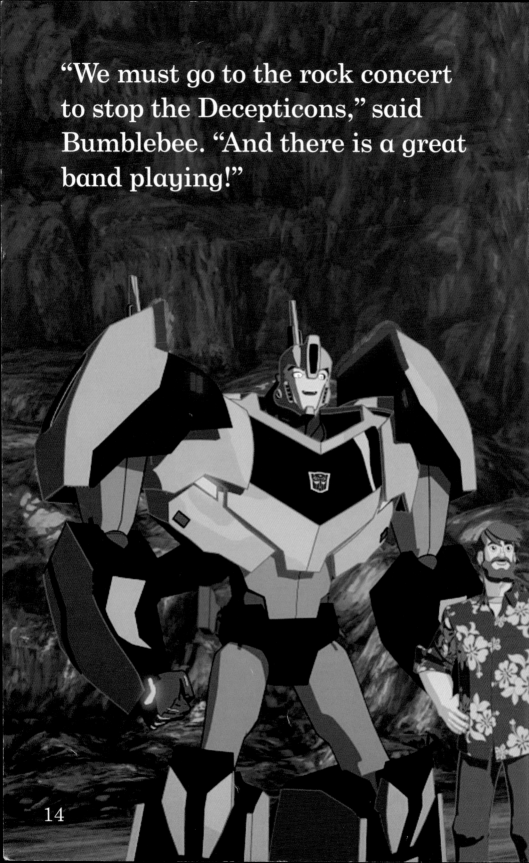

"I'd love to go to the rock concert, but I can't," said Denny. "Russell, you can go with Bumblebee. And get me a T-shirt, please!"

"But the music is boring!" said Russell.

On Saturday night, Bumblebee and Russell went to the Rumbledome.

Bumblebee stayed outside. He could hear the rock concert because the music was really loud! "The band is great!" he thought.

Russell went inside the Rumbledome to buy a T-shirt for Denny.

Russell bought the T-shirt.
Then, he went downstairs, where
he saw a Decepticon called Bisk,
and some other Decepticons!

"Oh no! They're taking a soundboard!" he thought.

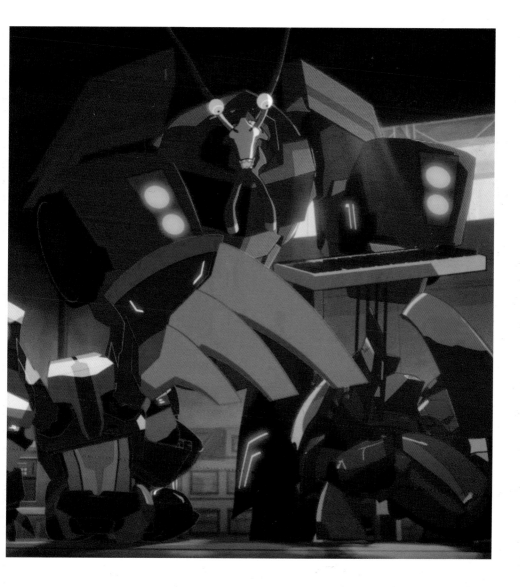

Then, Bisk saw Russell!
Russell ran very quickly,
and Bisk couldn't
catch him.

Russell ran outside to tell
Bumblebee about the Decepticons.

Bumblebee and Russell then went inside the Rumbledome to look for the Decepticons.

They went downstairs, but they couldn't find the Decepticons.

Russell had an idea. "Look, Bumblebee. You can go up there! Go and look for the Decepticons upstairs," he said.

Upstairs, Bumblebee could see the stage. He was very excited. "I can see the band!" he said.

Then, he saw Bisk walk on to the stage!

Bumblebee ran on to the stage, too. "I must stop him from taking the band's soundboard!" he thought.

The band was on the stage, too. They played their music and lots of people watched.

Russell watched, too.
"Oh no!" he thought. "All these
people can see Bumblebee!"

The people watched Bumblebee
and Bisk on the stage with
the band.

They thought Bumblebee and
Bisk were in the rock concert!

Some other Decepticons flew down and tried to catch Bumblebee.

But Bumblebee threw them at the
wall and they fell down.

Then, Bumblebee hit Bisk,
and he fell down, too.

It was the end of the rock concert, and everyone loved it.

Bumblebee and Russell put the Decepticons in a box, and they left the Rumbledome.

"I'm sorry you didn't see the rock concert," said Russell.

"But I was IN the rock concert," said Bumblebee. "That was better than watching it!"

Bumblebee and Russell took the Decepticons to the scrapyard.

"Well done!" said Strongarm, Grimlock, and Denny.

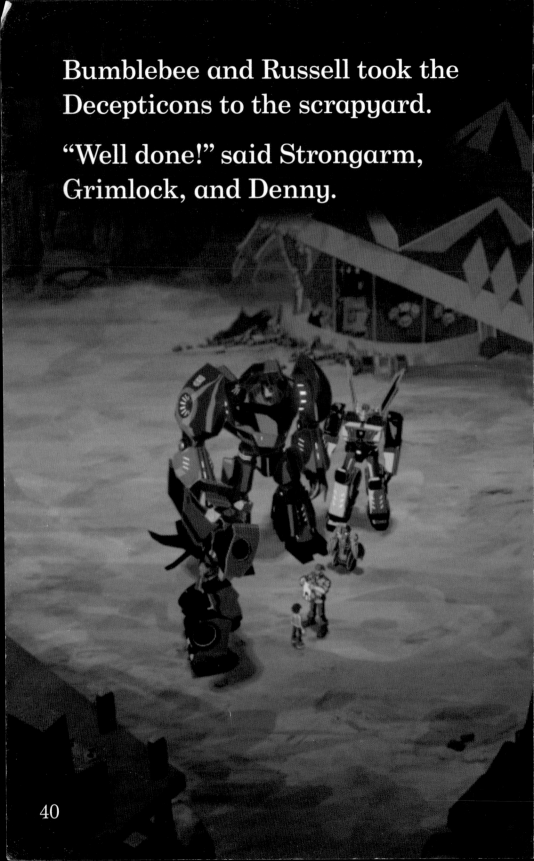

Russell gave Denny the T-shirt.

"I love it, thank you!" said Denny.

"Did you enjoy the rock concert?"
asked Denny.

"Oh, it was really boring . . ."
said Russell.

"Yes, it was a really boring night!" laughed Bumblebee.

Activities

The key below describes the skills practiced in each activity.

🖊️ Spelling and writing

📖 Reading

💬 Speaking

❓ Critical thinking

✴️ Preparation for the Cambridge Young Learners Exams

1 Look and read. Choose the correct words and write them on the lines.

T-shirt

rock concert

scrapyard

soundboard

1 There is lots of old metal here. _____scrapyard_____

2 People can wear this. _____

3 People who enjoy music like going to this. _____

4 People use this in rock concerts. _____

2 **Match the words to the pictures.**

1

a Bumblebee

2

b Strongarm

3

c Grimlock

4

d Denny

5

e Russell

6

f Fixit

3 Look and read. Write *yes* or *no*.

One Friday night, the Autobots were in the city, looking for Decepticons.

"The Decepticons want cables to get strong. We must find the cables. Then we can find the Decepticons and stop them," said Bumblebee.

1 The Autobots were in the city on Friday night.   <u>yes</u>

2 They wanted to find the cables.

3 Grimlock didn't find a cable in the train.

4 The Decepticons didn't take the cables.

5 Bumblebee wanted to find the cables, because then he could find the Decepticons.

4 Write the correct form of the verbs.

Grimlock looked in a train and found a cable.

But a Decepticon hit Grimlock and took it.

Bumblebee and Strongarm tried to catch the Decepticon, but he jumped on to a moving train.

"Ha, ha! I've got the cable!" he laughed.

9

1 Grimlock ___looked___ **(look)** in a train and found a cable.

2 But a Decepticon hit Grimlock and _____ **(take)** the cable.

3 Bumblebee and Strongarm _____ **(try)** to catch the Decepticon.

4 But he _____ **(jump)** on to a moving train.

5 "Ha, ha! I've got the cable!" he _____ **(laugh)**.

5 Write *because, but,* or *and*.

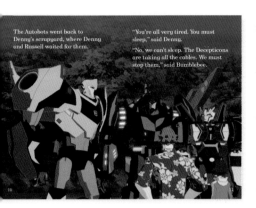

1 The robots were tired, ...**but**...... they didn't want to sleep.

2 They couldn't sleep, ... they were worried about the Decepticons.

3 The Decepticons had the cables .... Bumblebee wanted to stop them.

4 The Decepticons had cables, ... they didn't have soundboards.

5 Bumblebee wanted to go to the Rumbledome .... there are soundboards at rock concerts.

49

6 Look at the letters. Write the words.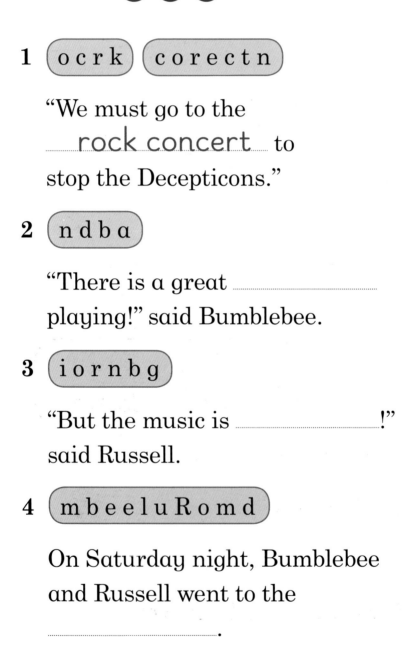

1 (o c r k) (c o r e c t n)

"We must go to the ___rock concert___ to stop the Decepticons."

2 (n d b a)

"There is a great _____ playing!" said Bumblebee.

3 (i o r n b g)

"But the music is _____!" said Russell.

4 (m b e e l u R o m d)

On Saturday night, Bumblebee and Russell went to the

_____.

7 **Ask and answer the questions with a friend.** 🗨 ❓

Russell bought the T-shirt. Then, he went downstairs, where he saw a Decepticon called Bisk, and some other Decepticons!

"Oh no! They're taking a soundboard!" he thought.

1 *Where is Russell?*

He's inside the Rumbledome.

2 What's he holding?

3 What can he hear?

4 What can he see?

5 How does he feel? Why?

8 Circle the correct words.

1 Russell went downstairs, **where** / **when** he saw a Decepticon called Bisk.

2 Russell was very **frightened** / **frightening** of Bisk.

3 This was because Bisk was very **frightened.** / **frightening.**

4 "Oh no! They **are taking** / **take** a soundboard!" Russell thought.

9 **Match the two parts of the sentences.** 📖

1 The Autobots went to the scrapyard

2 "We must go to the rock concert

3 Russell went inside

4 Russell ran outside

a the Rumbledome to buy a T-shirt.

b to see Denny and Russell.

c to stop the Decepticons," said Bumblebee.

d to tell Bumblebee about the Decepticons.

10 **Read the questions. Write the answers.**

1 Who was on the stage?

Bisk, Bumblebee, and the band.

2 What kind of concert was it?

3 Why did Bumblebee walk on to the stage?

4 How did the people feel about the concert, do you think?

11 **Look and read. Match the questions and answers.**

Bumblebee and Russell then went inside the Rumbledome to look for the Decepticons.

They went downstairs, but they couldn't find the Decepticons.

Then, Russell had an idea. "Look, Bumblebee. You can go up there. Go and look for the Decepticons upstairs," he said.

1 Who went downstairs in the Rumbledome? ....c........

2 Why did they go there? ....

3 What was Russell's idea? ....

a To look for the Decepticons.

b Bumblebee could look for the Decepticons upstairs.

c Bumblebee and Russell

12 **Write _T_ (true) or _F_ (false).**

Upstairs, Bumblebee could see the stage. He was very excited. "I can see the band!" he said.

Then, he saw Bisk walk on to the stage!

Bumblebee ran on to the stage, too. "I must stop him from taking the band's soundboard!" he thought.

The band was on the stage, too. They played their music and lots of people watched.

Russell watched, too. "Oh no!" he thought. "All these people can see Bumblebee!"

1 Upstairs, Bumblebee couldn't see the stage.   F

2 One of the Decepticons walked on the stage.

3 "I must stop him taking the soundboard," Russell thought.

4 The people at the rock concert couldn't see the band.

5 The people could see Bisk and Bumblebee on the stage.

13 **Read the text and choose the best answers.**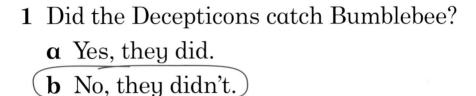

1 Did the Decepticons catch Bumblebee?

   a Yes, they did.

   b No, they didn't.

2 What did the Decepticons do after Bumblebee threw them at the wall?

   a They fell down.

   b They flew down.

3 What did the people think about Bumblebee and Bisk?

   a They were robots.

   b They were in the rock concert.

4 Who loved the rock concert?

   a The Decepticons loved it.

   b The people loved it.

14 **Read the text. Choose the correct words and write them on the lines.**

1	danced	ran	jumped
2	flew	threw	fell
3	flew	put	threw
4	put	hit	sat
5	took	hid	left

Bumblebee [1] _ran_ on to the stage.

Some Decepticons [2] _____ down

and tried to catch him. He [3] _____

the Decepticons at the wall. Then, he

[4] _____ Bisk. Later, Bumblebee

and Russell [5] _____ the

Decepticons to the scrapyard.

15 Who says this?

Russell

Denny

Strongarm

Bumblebee

1 "I'm sorry you didn't see the rock concert."   <u>Russell</u>

2 "But I was IN the rock concert!"   _____

3 "Well done!"   _____

4 "I love it, thank you!"   _____

16 Work with a friend. Ask and answer questions.

"Did you enjoy the rock concert?" asked Denny.

"Oh, it was really boring . . ." said Russell.

"Yes, it was a really boring night!" laughed Bumblebee.

1 *Why didn't Russell like the band?*

Because he thought the music was boring.

2 Why did Russell have to go to the rock concert?

3 Why did the people think Bumblebee and Bisk were in the rock concert?

4 Why does Bumblebee say, "Yes, it was a really boring night!"

17 Look at the pictures with a friend. One picture is different. How is it different? 💬 ❓

1 (a)  (b)  (c)

> *Picture c is different because Russell is inside.*

2 (a) 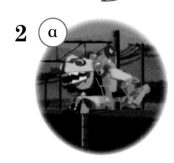 (b)  (c)

3 (a)  (b)  (c)

18 **Look and read. Write the correct words on the lines.**

> downstairs   upstairs
> inside   outside

1 Bumblebee stayed ....outside.... the Rumbledome.

2 Russell went .... the Rumbledome.

3 Then, he went .... where he saw the Decepticons.

4 Russell said to Bumblebee, "Go and look for the Decepticons ...."

19 Do the crossword.

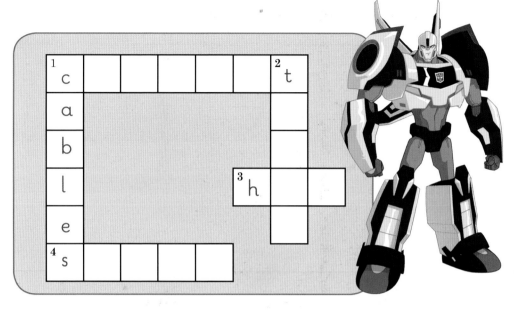

Down

1 The Decepticons wanted to take all the soundboards and . . .

2 A Decepticon jumped on to this.

Across

1 Bumblebee and Russell went to a rock . . .

3 Bumblebee . . . Bisk and he fell down.

4 The band, Bisk, and Bumblebee were on this.

Level 3

Sharks

978–0–241–25382–3 ☐

The Jungle Book

978–0–241–25383–0 ☐

The Red Knight

978–0–241–25384–7 ☐

The Elves and the Shoemaker

978–0–241–25385–4 ☐

Rapunzel

978–0–241–28394–3 ☐

Great Buildings

978–0–241–28400–1 ☐

Minibeasts

978–0–241–28404–9 ☐

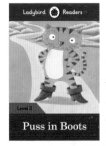

Puss in Boots

978–0–241–28407–0 ☐

Jack and the Beanstalk

978–0–241–28397–4 ☐

Hansel and Gretel

978–0–241–29861–9 ☐

The Talent Show

978–0–241–29859–6 ☐

A Great Night!

978-0-241-29863-3 ☐

Bumblebee and the Rock Concert

978-0-241-29867-1 ☐

Where Animals Live

978-0-241-29868-8 ☐

Now you're ready for Level 4!